YOUR KNOWLEDGE HAS VALUE

- We will publish your bachelor's and master's thesis, essays and papers

- Your own eBook and book - sold worldwide in all relevant shops

- Earn money with each sale

Upload your text at www.GRIN.com and publish for free

Sukayna El-Zayat

Al-Jazeera as a tool for Qatari foreign policy?

GRIN Verlag

Bibliografische Information der Deutschen Nationalbibliothek:

Die Deutsche Bibliothek verzeichnet diese Publikation in der Deutschen Nationalbibliografie; detaillierte bibliografische Daten sind im Internet über http://dnb.d-nb.de/ abrufbar.

Dieses Werk sowie alle darin enthaltenen einzelnen Beiträge und Abbildungen sind urheberrechtlich geschützt. Jede Verwertung, die nicht ausdrücklich vom Urheberrechtsschutz zugelassen ist, bedarf der vorherigen Zustimmung des Verlages. Das gilt insbesondere für Vervielfältigungen, Bearbeitungen, Übersetzungen, Mikroverfilmungen, Auswertungen durch Datenbanken und für die Einspeicherung und Verarbeitung in elektronische Systeme. Alle Rechte, auch die des auszugsweisen Nachdrucks, der fotomechanischen Wiedergabe (einschließlich Mikrokopie) sowie der Auswertung durch Datenbanken oder ähnliche Einrichtungen, vorbehalten.

Imprint:

Copyright © 2012 GRIN Verlag GmbH
Druck und Bindung: Books on Demand GmbH, Norderstedt Germany
ISBN: 978-3-656-34657-9

This book at GRIN:

http://www.grin.com/en/e-book/206627/al-jazeera-as-a-tool-for-qatari-foreign-policy

GRIN - Your knowledge has value

Der GRIN Verlag publiziert seit 1998 wissenschaftliche Arbeiten von Studenten, Hochschullehrern und anderen Akademikern als eBook und gedrucktes Buch. Die Verlagswebsite www.grin.com ist die ideale Plattform zur Veröffentlichung von Hausarbeiten, Abschlussarbeiten, wissenschaftlichen Aufsätzen, Dissertationen und Fachbüchern.

Visit us on the internet:

http://www.grin.com/

http://www.facebook.com/grincom

http://www.twitter.com/grin_com

- ASSIGNMENT 4 -
First Draft

Al-Jazeera as a tool of Qatari foreign policy?

Sukayna El-Zayat
Date: 18-10-12
Assignment 4
Final Version

Introduction

Since its first appearance, the Arabic network of Al-Jazeera has been the target of many different critics. Some say, the channel supports terrorism; others praise it as the first free and independent Arab media.

Al-Jazeera has been funded by Qatar since its beginning and it is now led by a member of the Qatari royal family; the question which then arises is whether Al-Jazeera is as independent as it claims.

This paper analyses the relationship between Qatar and Al-Jazeera. Therefore, firstly Qatar's foreign affairs and interests are presented, and then a comparative analysis of Al-Jazeera's coverage of the Arab spring follows. My thesis states that Al-Jazeera functions as an instrument for Qatari foreign policy or is at least heavily influenced by it and is consequently not able to present balanced reporting independently. Using the examples of Libya and Bahrain, this essay shows that the tendencies of Al-Jazeera's coverage match the respective tone of Qatar's foreign policy. Additionally, it looks more deeply at the replacement of Wadah Khanfar, ex-director of Al-Jazeera who has been replaced by a member of the Qatari royal family.

Al-Jazeera

Al-Jazeera is an Arab broadcast network which unites several different channels under its roof, the two best known being the news channels Al-Jazeera Arabic and Al-Jazeera English. News is additionally distributed over a live stream on Al-Jazeera's website, a YouTube channel and Twitter. The original Arabic channel was launched 1st November, 1996 – the English sister followed ten years later. Both are broadcasted to more than 100 countries, mainly the Arab-speaking part of the World and reach a viewership up to 220 million (Al Jazeera English, 2003). At the networks first emergence it was broadly received as an alternative to the rest of the Arab media, which was up to this point state-controlled and therefore heavily censored. Al-Jazeera is owned by the Emir of Qatar, Sheikh Hamad bin Thamer/bin Khalifa Al-Thani who has granted the network a start-up of $137 million US dollars (Miles, Al-Jazeera: How Arab TV news challenged the world, 2005). In the following years "hundreds of millions of dollars annually" [Al-Jazeera's Washington bureau chief Abderrahim Foukara (Tharoor, 2011)] were invested by the Emir.

Corresponding to their motto "The opinion and the opposing opinion", Al-Jazeera set up a code of ethics which indicates balanced and independent reporting as well as the guarantee that no political priority should be held over the professional one.

Qatar and its foreign policy

The state of Qatar is situated on the Arab Peninsula; it shares a border with Saudi-Arabia, apart from that it is surrounded by the Persian Gulf. Qatar gained independence in 1971, before that it had been a British Protectorate. Since then, the country has been ruled by the Al-Thani clan, the current head of state being Sheikh Hamad bin Khalifa Al-Thani. Although Qatar is ruled as an absolute hereditary emirate, it has been the first country in the Gulf region to hold democratic elections over certain authorities within the regime. Being a rather rich state, Qatar counts a GDP of $182.004 million – this has its roots primarily in oil resources and extensive fields of natural gas.

Miles compares the ruling emir to "a managing director, running a large corporation" (Miles, Al-Jazeera: How Arab TV news challenged the world, 2005); indeed Sheikh Hamad has been very forward in pushing his 'trademark' Qatar to an important position on the world board. In addition, he takes a stand for women's emancipation, resulting in their right to vote, to drive without company and to take part in the Olympics. Those achievements may seem self-evident to a Westerner, even the Muslim ones, but in the region they are rather rare. Furthermore, he established a very high standard of education in Qatar and he campaigns freedom of speech and press, with the establishment of Al-Jazeera as his showpiece. Though his activities clearly modernized the country, no political parties or any other kind of opposition to the regime are tolerated. This means that Qatar's accomplishments in recent years depend on the current emir, who happens to have progressive and agreeable interests which he follows. If a descendant, and therefore a future emir would think differently, Qatar might not be able to sustain its open-minded position.

Qatar's foreign policy has been summarized by Miles as consistently "trying to get along with everyone" (Miles, Al-Jazeera: How Arab TV news challenged the world, 2005). This is quite accurate since three types of stabilization are the main goal of Qatar; first the stabilization of Qatar's position worldwide, second stabilizing the current emir's ruling position within Qatar and third the stabilization of Qatar's region.

Sheikh Hamad stated that his country "should be 'known and noticed'" (Miles, Al-Jazeera: How Arab TV news challenged the world, 2005). This thought is mirrored for example in the fact that Qatar is the only Arab state in the region not having diplomatic, but at least commercial relations with Israel (Cafiero, 2012). Moreover, Qatar hosts the largest US military base of the region, consequently ensuring the cooperation of the U.S. (Akhmetov, 2012). Hence, secure and peaceful ties with all the 'global players' are important for Qatar's Emir.

Concerning regional stability, Qatar engages in foreign cooperation and diplomacy in order to secure its economic interests; as its most important trade route to Asia goes through the Strait of Hormuz (sea passage connecting the Persian Gulf to the Arabian Sea). Sharing a natural gas area with Iran, Qatar has established a security agreement with Tehran. After having territorial disagreements with Saudi-Arabia, Qatar applied several diplomatic initiatives to strengthen the relationship. In addition, Qatar has served as a mediator in Yemen during the civil war, in Gaza after the parliamentary elections and in Lebanon's upheaving in 2008.

Compared to its rather small size, Qatar exercises a very ambitious and proactive policy. This originates in the country's problematic domestic affairs (Akhmetov, 2012), as the new Qatari Emir was anxious to present a positive image, facing rejection by Saudi-Arabia and Egypt after his coup d'état (Hroub, 2011). The emir's position is primarily endangered through his own family; therefore Sheikh Hamad establishes security agreements with as many globally important countries as possible (Kamrava, 2009).

The question of sustainability emerges given the difficult balancing act Qatar performs as Senator Kelly puts it in 2009: "Qatar cannot continue to be an American ally on Monday that sends money to Hamas on Tuesday." (Cafiero, 2012).

Al-Jazeera's coverage of Libya and Bahrain during the Arab Spring in comparison

When NATO intervened militarily in Libya during its revolution in'March, 2011, Qatar was the first Arab state to take part (Cafiero, 2012). Libyan rebels were armed and heavily funded with $400 million by the Qatari government (Eakin, 2011). Additionally, Qatar sent parts of its own special forces to train and support the opposition. As the Libyan rebels finally defeated Gaddafi, they even "raised a Qatari flag in appreciation" (Hounshell, Foreign Policy, 2012). Libya was not the only revolution of the Arab Spring in which Qatar took a rather active role; it was strongly involved in Egypt and Syria as well.

This policy is strongly mirrored in Al-Jazeera's coverage of the events. Since the beginning of the revolution, the channel has been focusing on Libyan revolutionaries and was "clearly Anti-Gaddafi" (Interview with Hashem, 2012). Schechter states that the "coverage has not been as sharp as it used to in other contexts" (Schechter, 2011). Al-Jazeera moved the slots of their usual programs and shortened the time for advertisements, in order to be able to offer extensive, daily reporting on the Libyan revolution. Blake Hounshell goes as far as to summarize the Libyan coverage as "utterly over-the-top, enthusiastic cheerleading for the rebels" (Hounshell, Foreign Policy, 2011).

One could argue that the Libyan rebels needed that coverage to overcome Gaddafi as a ruling dictator and that in fact a more neutral coverage would in this case be unfair, as the oppositions was much weaker and had fewer possibilities than the regime. Still, Al-Jazeera gave opinion rather than information, a fact which stands in contrast to their slogan; claiming to always provide 'the opinion and the opposing one'. The network consequently made it more difficult for its viewers to make up their own mind about the events.

The case of Bahrain looks very similar, but the other way round; here Qatar's interest to keep its neighborhood stabilized and safe lead to an extreme lack of coverage from Al-Jazeera. As Hashem, an ex-reporter for Al-Jazeera puts it: "It was clear that Gulf-financed stations were more interested in regional security than Bahrainis' dreams of democracy and freedom and their revolt against tyranny." (Hashem, 2012). Every revolution of the Arab Spring has been openly offered and provided with support by Qatar and the network, "other than in Bahrain where the Saudis and, more pointedly, the Americans drew a very sharp red line." (Hroub, 2011). This makes it very clear that the Qatari regime indeed took Al-Jazeera as an instrument for its foreign interests – stabilizing the diplomatic ties with their allies. When the Bahraini regime violently suppressed the protest and demonstrations in the country, Qatar supported this measure by sending their own troops for assistance (Eakin, 2011).

It is evident that Al-Jazeera applied a double standard when reporting on the events of the Arab Spring; Miles states that "ever since the start of the Arab spring, Al-Jazeera's coverage has been patchy" (Patel, 2012).

Wadah Khanfar

Wadah Khanfar has been the director general of Al-Jazeera for eight years. On 20th September he unexpectedly resigned and left the network (Miles, BBC News, 2011). Wadah Khanfar has been linked to a cable from the US embassy which reports that in 2005, he agreed to tone down critical articles concerning the Iraq War (Eakin, 2011). Moreover, the cable presents Al-Jazeera as a "bargaining tool [for Qatar's foreign affairs] to repair relationships with other countries" (the guardian, 2010). After his resignation, Khanfar stated in an interview broadcasted on Al-Jazeera itself, that the reason for his departure was simply that he "decided to move on" (Al-Jazeera English, 2011). However, Miles indicates that he was rather "asked to leave by the royal family" (Miles, BBC News, 2011). This statement is especially convincing, if one looks more closely at his replacement. Sheikh Ahmed Al-Thani, a member of the royal family, is the new director general, though he has no journalistic experiences and qualifications but comes from a commercial background, as he was the executive of Qatar's biggest natural gas corporation (Hounshell, Foreign Policy, 2011). This means that Al-Jazeera is not only financially supported by Qatar, but that the content matter is now officially in royal hands as well.

Conclusion

There is no doubt that Al Jazeera has been one of the most important catalysts and change facilitators in the Arab world during the last one and a half decades and it has tremendously supported the awakening of the region to an extent that has shaken the whole political landscape after a long time of oppression and stagnancy. Some say that Al-Jazeera's appearance has been the most critical turning point to the Arab world since the empowerment of Gamal Abdel-Nasser. Former Egyptian president Mubarak had the opportunity to visit Al Jazeera during a stay in Qatar and was astonished about the small size of the building. He then was quoted to say, "So this is the matchbox that sets the whole region in fire?" (Miles, Al-Jazeera: How Arab TV news challenged the world, 2005) Indeed Al Jazeera has been one of the key players in regime change in Egypt.

Even if Al-Jazeera has been reporting for more than a decade relatively free and independent this has certainly changed during the last three years.

Taking especially the recent events of the Arab Spring into account, it can be clearly stated that Al-Jazeera's reporting of the revolutions was partly biased and unbalanced. Furthermore, it reflected to a relevant extent the respective policy of Qatar on the preferred outcome of the revolution. That means, that Al-Jazeera's freedom reaches only as far as the Emir allows. As long as Qatar is ruled by a relative modern and open regime, the same goes for the network. What remains unclear is what would happen if that given situation changes.

However, without the heavy coverage of for example the Egyptian revolution by Al-Jazeera, the situation of Egypt could likely be worse now. Al-Jazeera brought attention to the situation and most importantly, since herein lies the difference to the mainstream western media, it constantly kept reminding its viewers of the events so that the instable situations would not be forgotten by the societies who were not directly concerned.

Even though, Al-Jazeera is not independent from Qatar, this does not mean that they do not provide 'good' reporting. There are no neutral or completely independent news agencies, as everyone has evidently their own agendas which they try to follow and support. The problem is that these agencies still claim to have the possibility to report freely. However, the dependence of the networks must be presented more transparent to the public, so that news and background information is provided in a more reflected manner. As Luyendijk suggests, there has to be some kind of journalism about journalism; meaning that journalistic challenges and the lack of thorough knowledge must be taken in account and made public along with the actual news (Luyendijk, 2006).

I conclude with Miles' statement that Al-Jazeera must be judged realistically since "all news channels are biased. Al-Jazeera is not better or worse than any other station." (Miles, Al-Jazeera: How Arab TV news challenged the world, 2005).

Bibliography

Al Jazeera English. (2003). Abgerufen am 15. October 2012 von http://www.aljazeera.com/aboutus/2010/11/20101110131438787482.html

the guardian. (5. December 2010). Abgerufen am 15. October 2012 von US embassy cables: Qatar using al-Jazeera as bargaining tool, claims US: http://www.guardian.co.uk/world/us-embassy-cables-documents/235574

Al-Jazeera English. (21. September 2011). Abgerufen am 15. October 2012 von Al Jazeera's Khanfar on why he stepped down: http://www.aljazeera.com/video/middleeast/2011/09/2011921121515194101.html

Akhmetov, T. (27. February 2012). *openDemocracy.* Abgerufen am 15. October 2012 von Explaining Qatar's foreign policy: http://www.opendemocracy.net/timur-akhmetov/explaining-qatars-foreign-policy-0

Cafiero, G. (25. June 2012). *Foreign Policy in focus.* Abgerufen am 15. October 2012 von Is Qatar's foreign policy sustainable?: http://www.fpif.org/articles/is_qatars_foreign_policy_sustainable

Eakin, H. (27. October 2011). *The New York Review of Books.* Abgerufen am 15. October 2012 von The Strange Power of Qatar: http://www.nybooks.com/articles/archives/2011/oct/27/strange-power-qatar/?pagination=false

Hashem, A. (3. April 2012). *the guardian.* Abgerufen am 15. October 2012 von The Arab spring has shaken Arab TV's credibility: http://www.guardian.co.uk/commentisfree/2012/apr/03/arab-spring-arab-tv-credibility

Hounshell, B. (20. September 2011). *Foreign Policy.* Abgerufen am 15. October 2012 von The End of the Al-Jazeera decade?: http://blog.foreignpolicy.com/posts/2011/09/20/the_end_of_the_al_jazeera_decade

Hounshell, B. (May/June 2012). *Foreign Policy.* Abgerufen am 15. October 2012 von The Qatar Bubble: http://www.foreignpolicy.com/articles/2012/04/23/the_qatar_bubble?page=0,1

Hroub, K. (Autumn 2011). *Europe's world.* Abgerufen am 15. October 2012 von How Al-Jazeera's Arab spring advanced Qatar's foreign policies: http://www.europesworld.org/NewEnglish/Home_old/Article/tabid/191/ArticleType/ArticleView/ArticleID/21877/language/en-us/HowAlJazeerasArabspringadvancedQatarsforeignpolicies.aspx

Interview with Hashem, A. (21. March 2012). *The Real News.* Abgerufen am 15. October 2012 von Former Al Jazeera Reporter on Libyan Coverage: http://therealnews.com/t2/index.php?option=com_content&task=view&id=31&Itemid=74&jumival=8107

Kamrava, M. (2009). *Royal Factionalism and Political Liberalization in Qatar.* The Middle East Journal.

Luyendijk, J. (2006). *People like us: Misrepresenting the Middle East.* New York: Soft Skull Press.

Miles, H. (1. October 2011). *BBC News.* Abgerufen am 15. October 2012 von Al-Jazeera boss steps down: strains with Qatar royals?: http://www.bbc.co.uk/news/world-middle-east-15129440?print=true

Miles, H. (2005). *Al-Jazeera: How Arab TV news challenged the world.* London, Great Britain: Abacus (Little, Brown Book Group).

Patel, K. (13. August 2012). *Daily Maverick.* Abgerufen am 15. October 2012 von Is Al-Jazeera a shill for Qatari foreign policy?: http://dailymaverick.co.za/article/2012-08-13-is-al-jazeera-a-shrill-for-qatari-foreign-policy

Schechter, D. (2. September 2011). Al-Jazeera - biased coverage of Libya and Syria? http://www.youtube.com/watch?feature=player_embedded&v=Z0TiAH_1LnA#!

Tharoor, I. (22. February 2011). *TIME magazine.* Abgerufen am 15. October 2012 von Why the U.S. needs Al-Jazeera: http://www.time.com/time/nation/article/0,8599,2052934,00.html

Booth and Rawlins & Metzger as accompanying literature

I found that both books were very easy to read and to understand. Especially Rawlins & Metzger offered practical tips and advice on organizing both; the research as well as the part of actually writing the paper. They provided vivid examples to make the text more readable.

In chapter eight of Rawlins & Metzgers "The Writer's Way" they refer to the importance of the tone and its relationship to the intended audience. After having read that chapter, I changed certain sentences of my first draft where I expressed myself in a too extreme manner. The authors state that the 'wrong' tone can undermine ones other wisely strong argument, so I tried to tone down my reasoning and make it more distant.

Moreover, in Chapter Seventeen, they argue about the reasons for including sources and when to quote. This helped me to revise all my quotes, in order to see whether they are fundamentally important to support my argument and whether the specific wording is substantial.

Booth highlights the importance of a clear claim. In Chapter eight of his book "The Craft of Research" he explains what a 'good' claim consists of and that a claim should never be vague. Following his instructions, I revised my own claim and included a very clear statement which is supported by my reasons and evidence. I think that this helps to give the paper a specific purpose – to justify your claim as well as to convince your readers of it.